Seasons

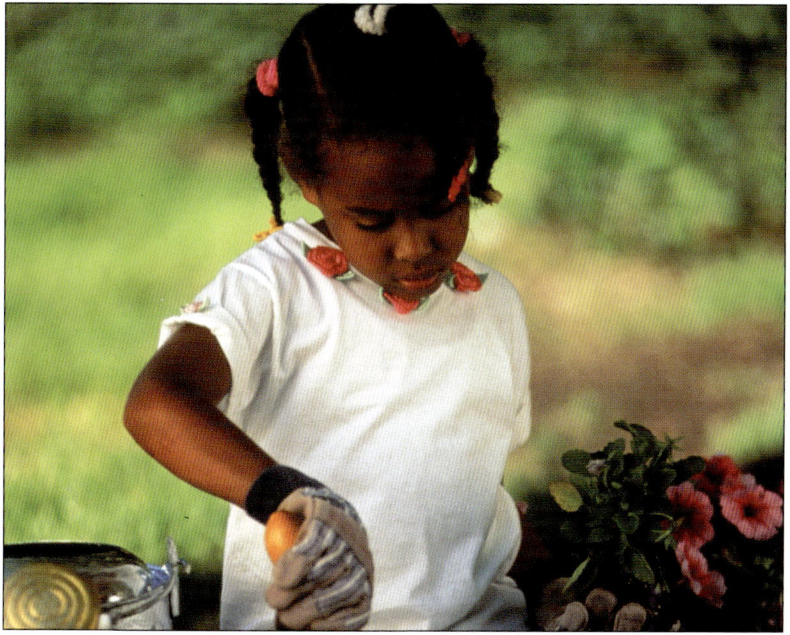

Christine Finochio • Jennette MacKenzie

Fall is here.

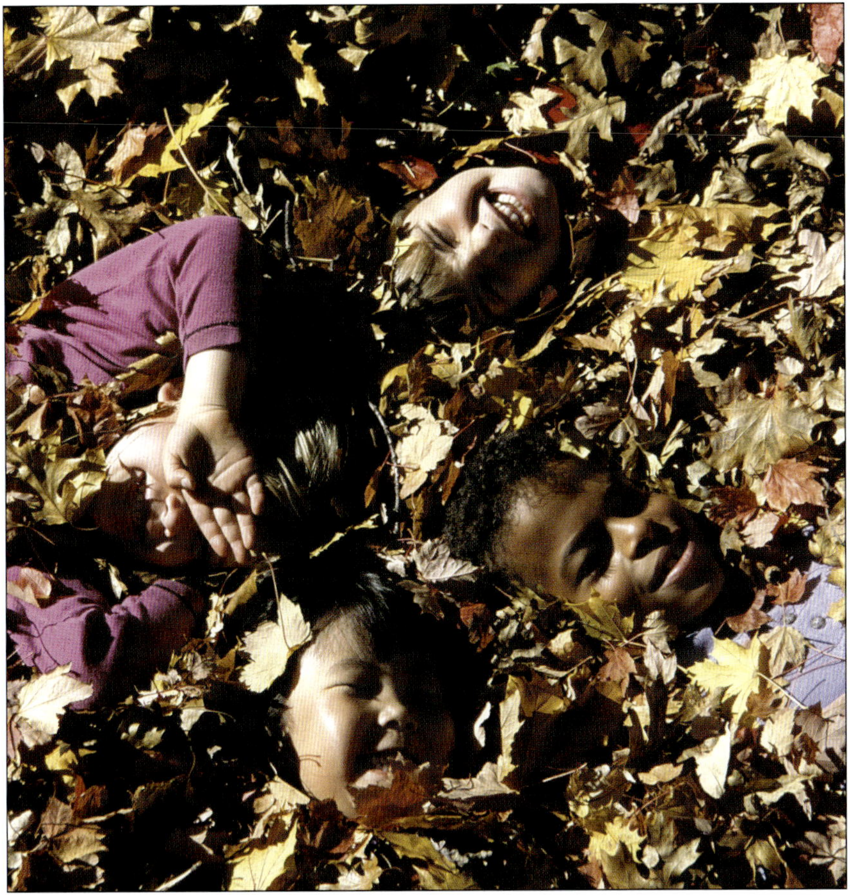

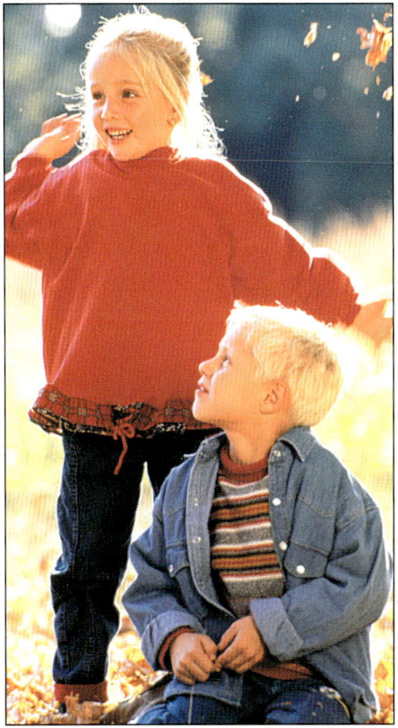

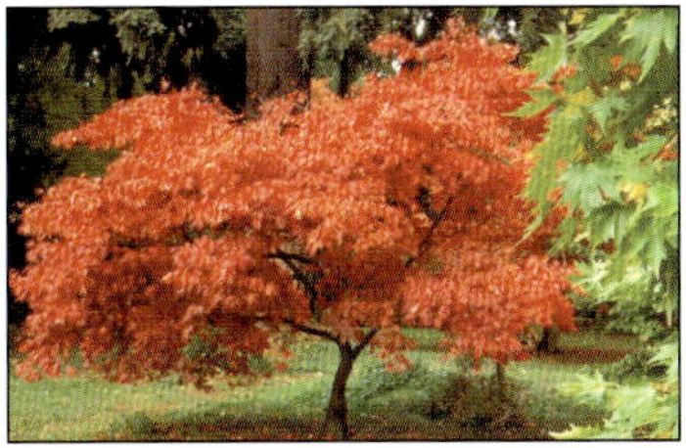

I am raking.

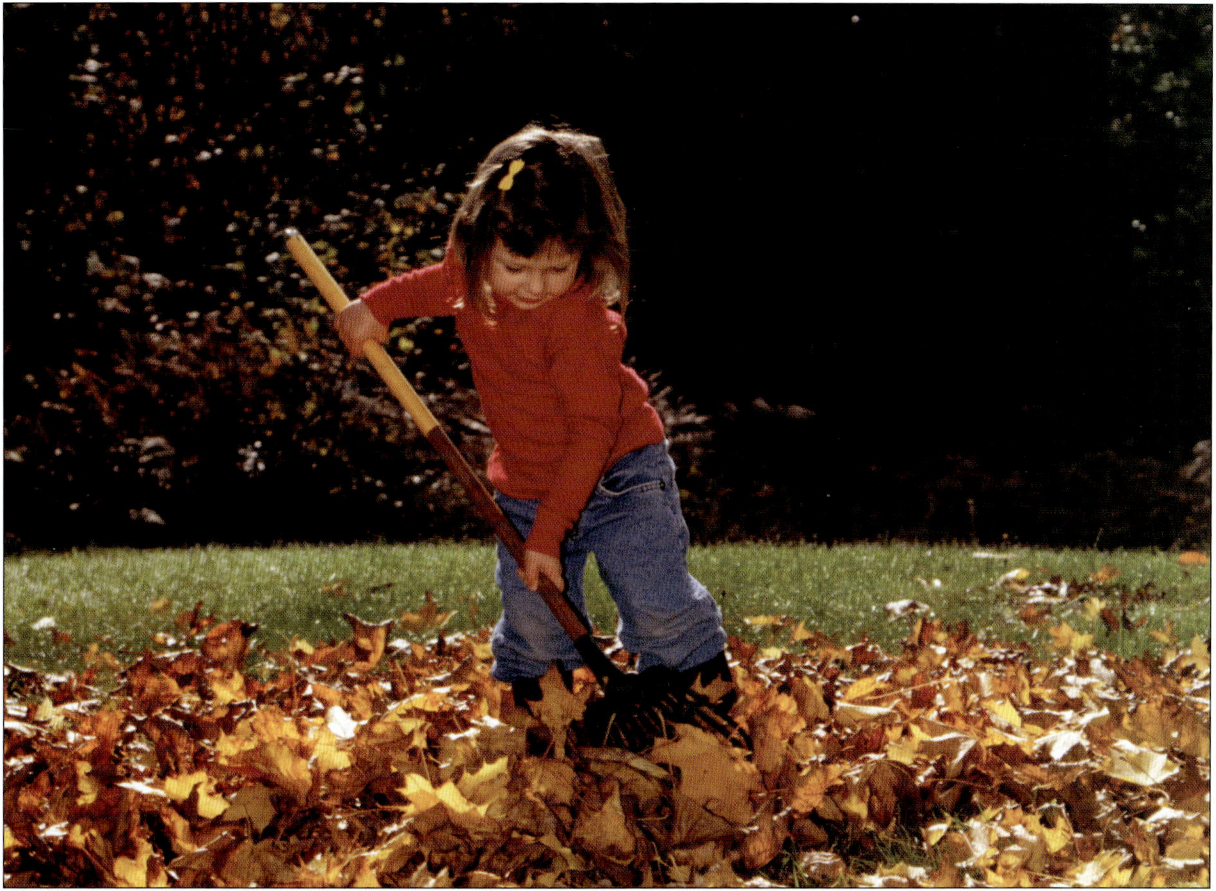

Winter is here.

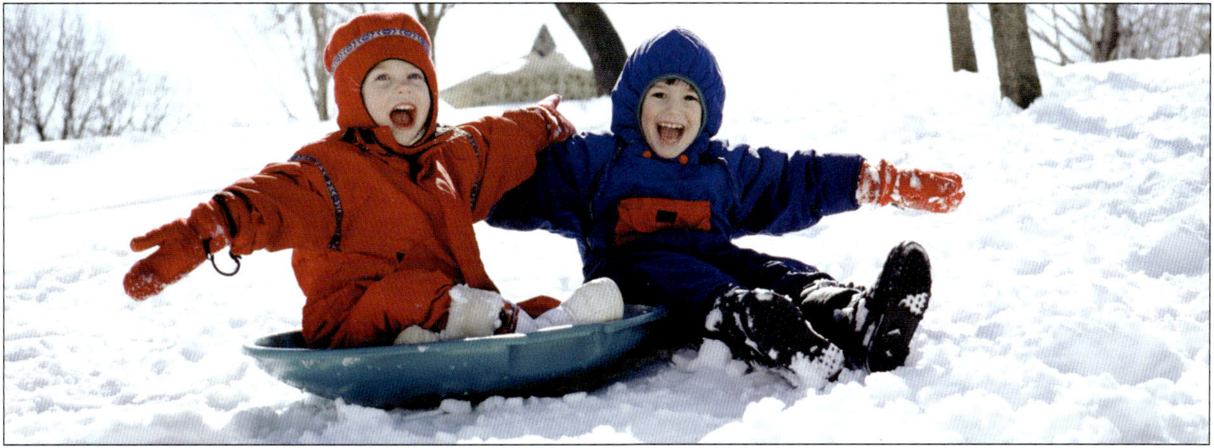

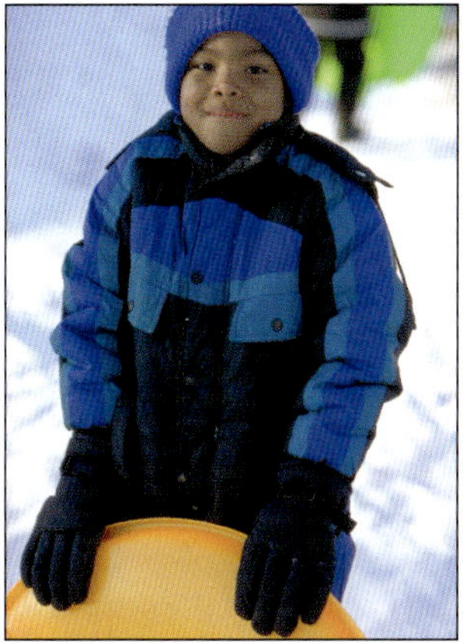

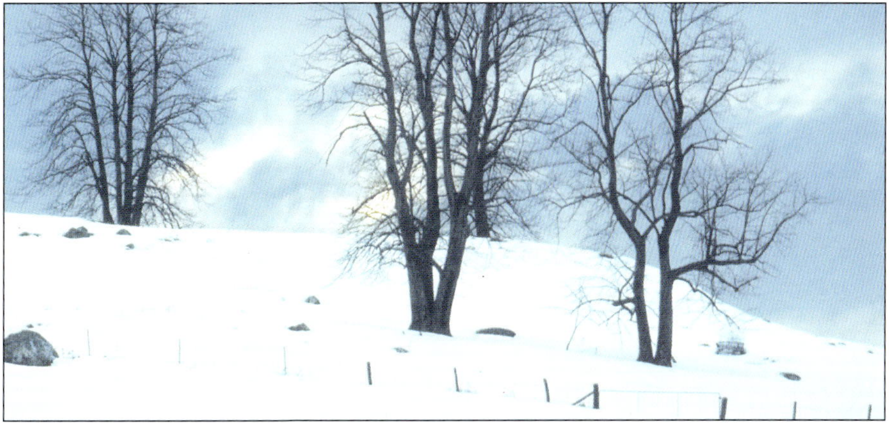

I am shoveling.

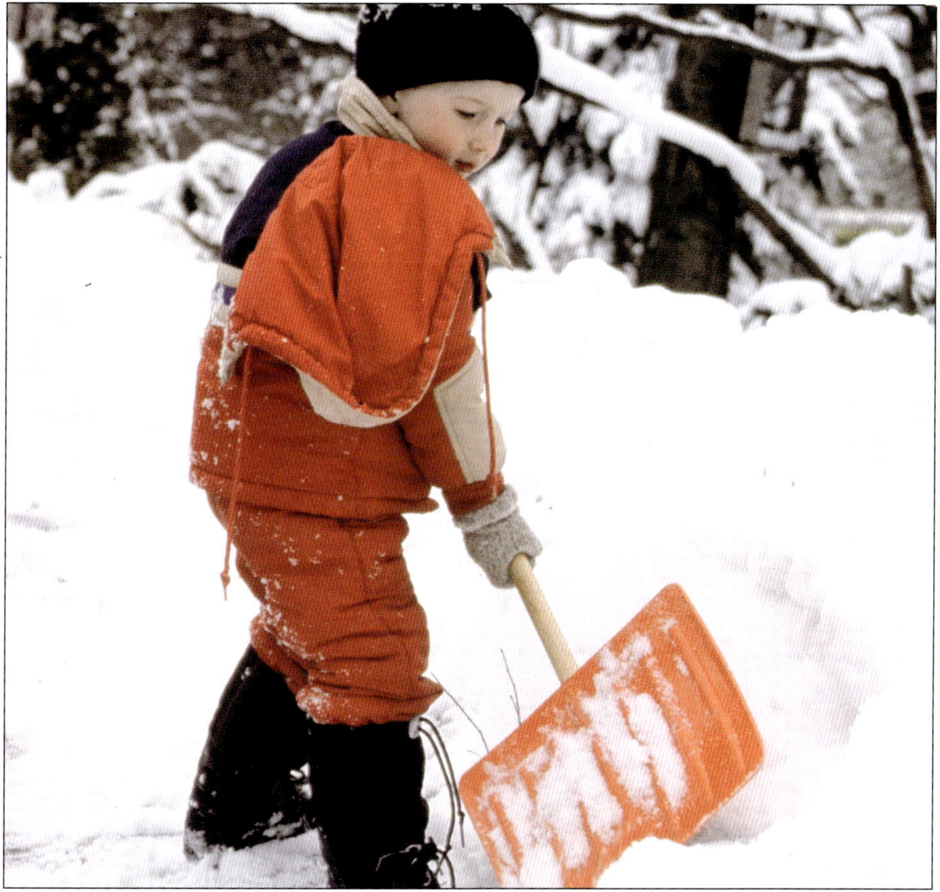

Spring is here.

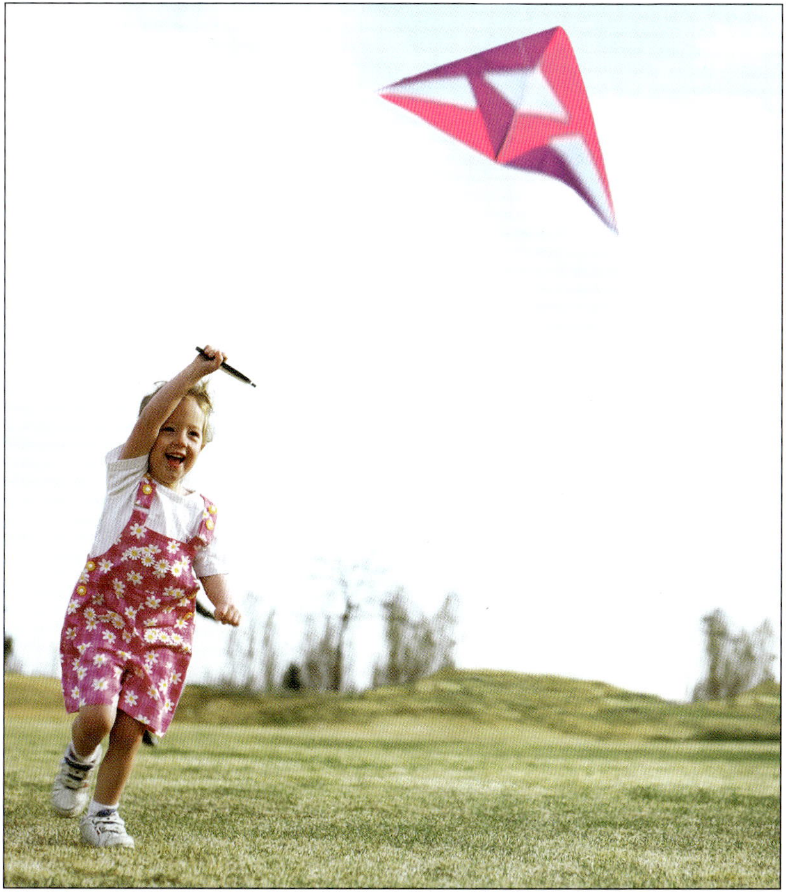

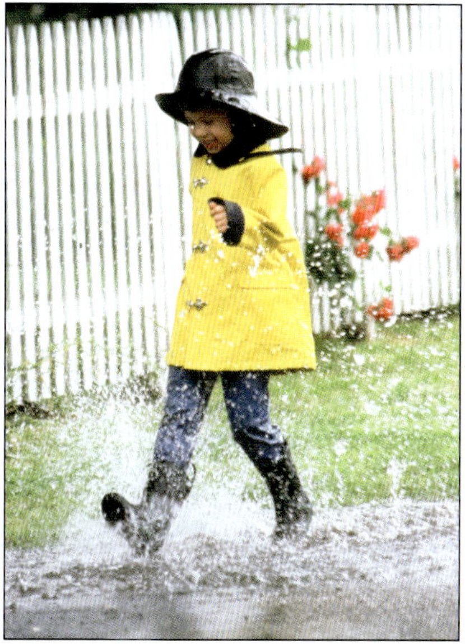

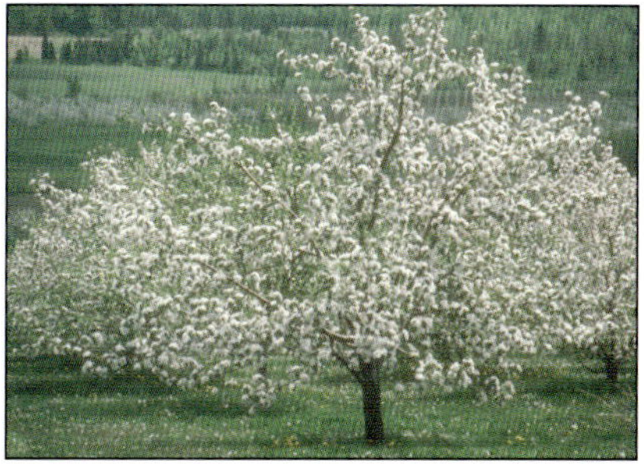

I am planting.

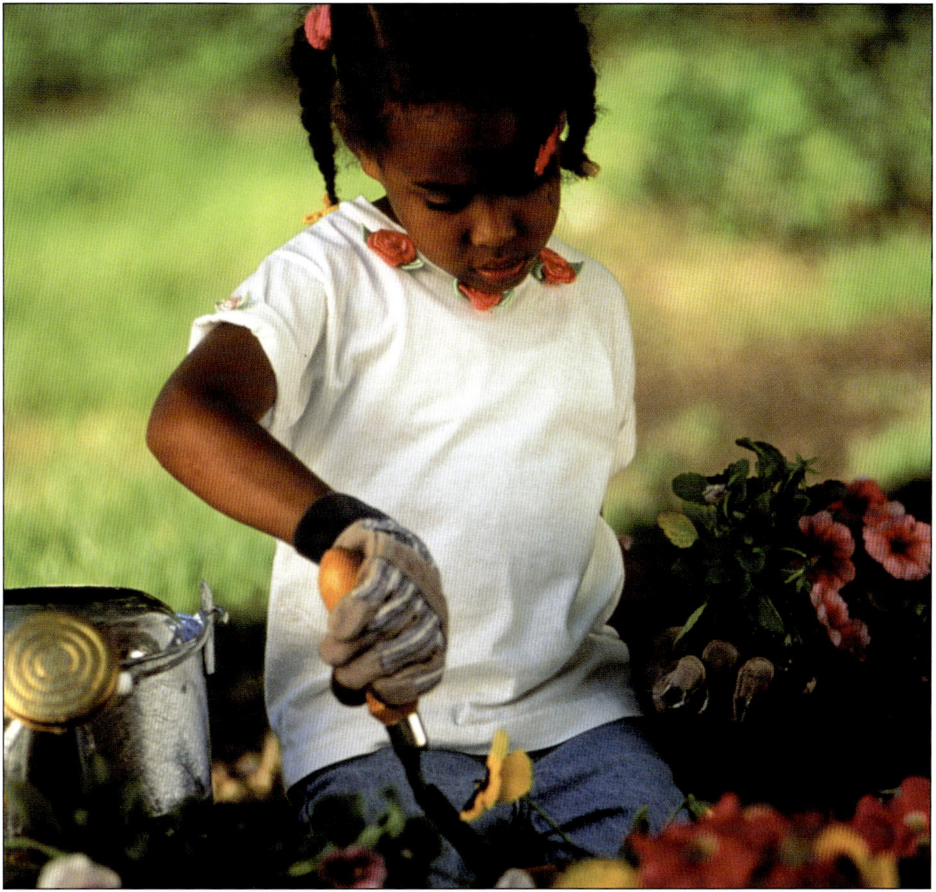

Summer is here.

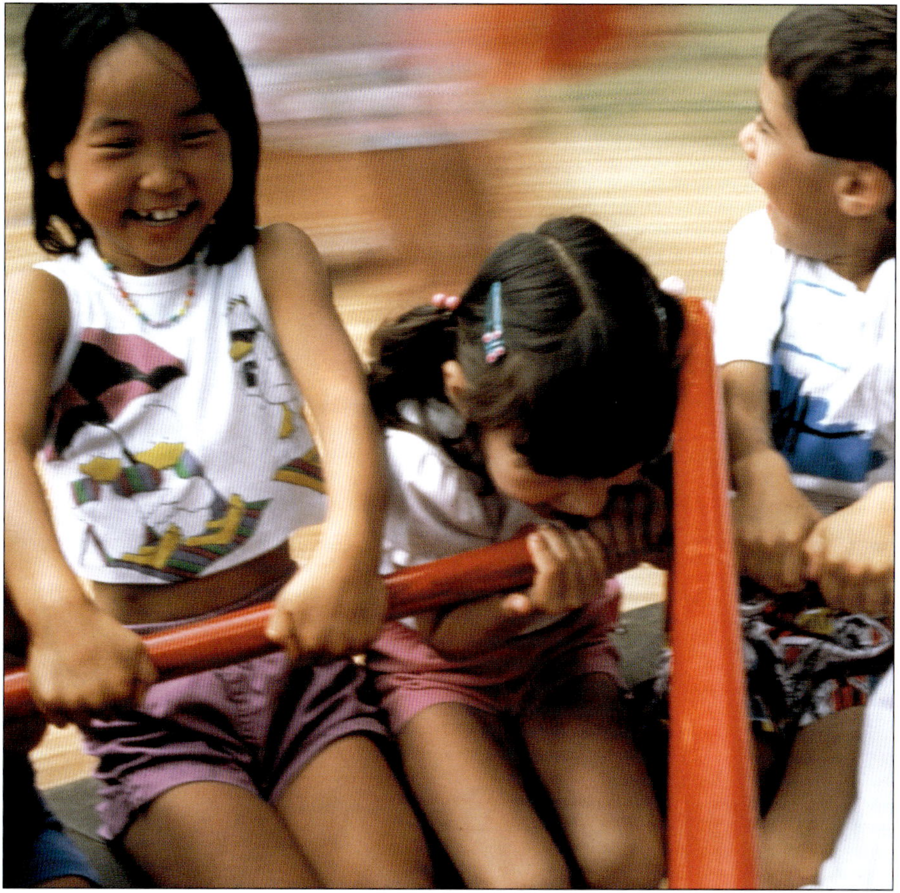
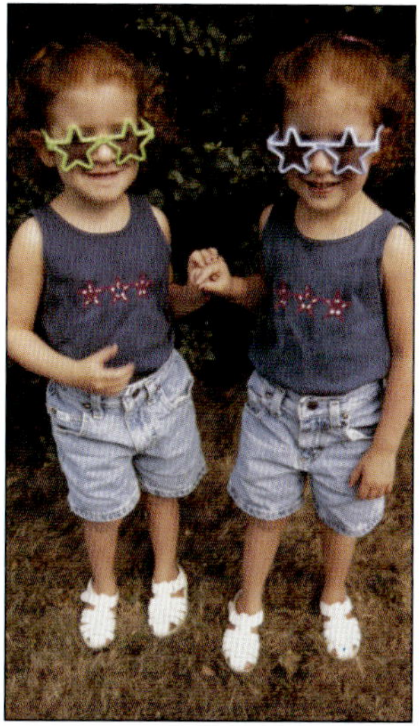
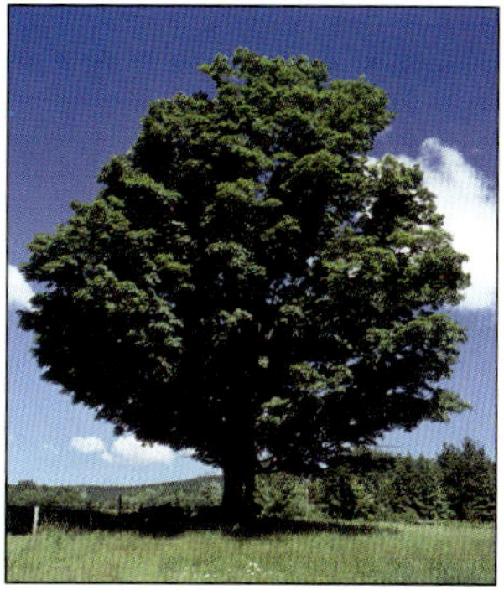

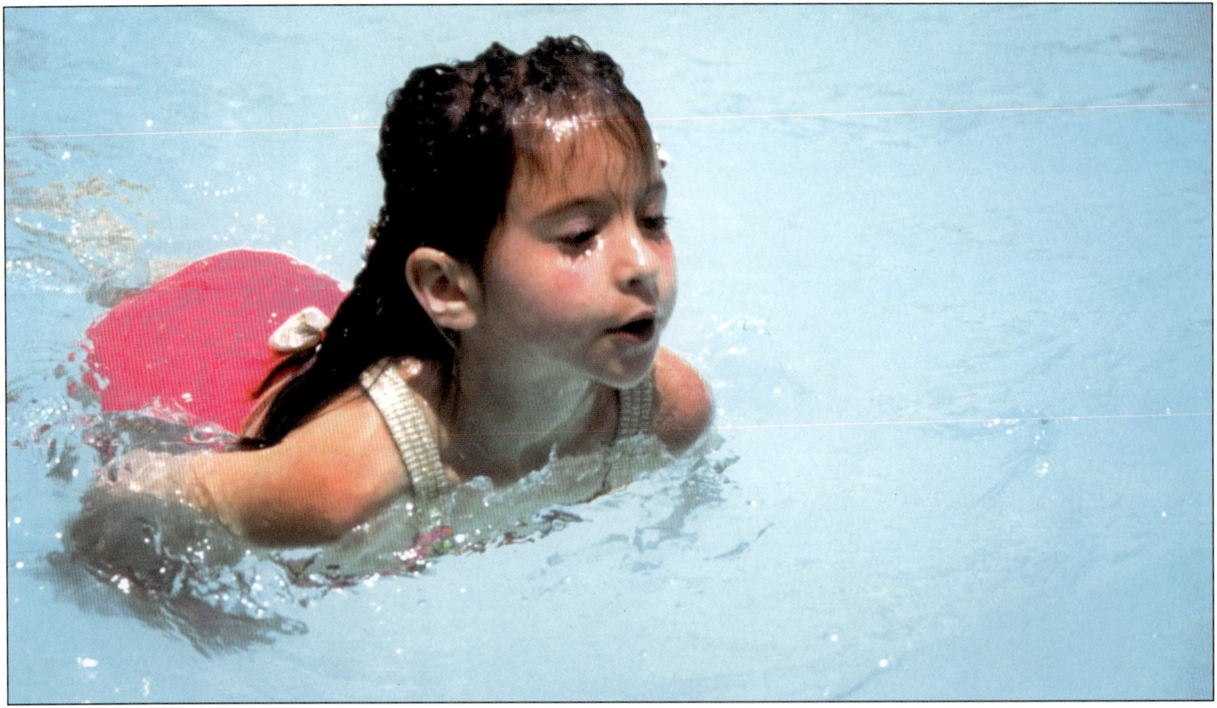

I am swimming.